THE DANCE OF YELLOW LIGHTNING OVER THE RIDGE

JIM COHN

Writers & Books Publications
Rochester, New York

ALSO BY JIM COHN

Poetry

Green Sky (1980)
Prairie Falcon (1989)
Grasslands (1994)

Letters

Coming Clean (1987)
[correspondence with Randy Roark]

Recordings

The Road (1995)
Walking Thru Hell Gazing At Flowers (1996)
Unspoken Words (1998)

First views of some of these poems appeared in the following small press publications to which the author wishes to express his gratitude: *Big Hammer, Big Scream, Desperate Acts, Friction, HazMat, Long Shot, Napalm Health Spa* & the *Paterson Literary Review.*

Acknowledgement also to these poets of my time: Sam Abrams, Antler, Todd Beers, Andy Clausen, Jack Collom, David Cope, Carol Graser, Bobby Johnson, Gary Lawless, Marc Olmsted, Tom Peters, Debbie Rennie, Sue Rhynhart, Joe Richey, Bob Rixon, Randy Roark, Shira Segal, Anne Waldman, Neil Young & the ghost of Allen Ginsberg.

THE DANCE OF YELLOW LIGHTNING OVER THE RIDGE: POEMS 1993-1997.

FIRST EDITION

Cover art designed by Ellen Orleans.

ISBN: 0-9618487-4-X

Writers & Books Publications
Rochester, New York

Table of Contents

THE PLACE NO ONE KNEW

RED BUTEO'D HEART

YUCCA MOUNTAIN

DELUGE SHELTER

WILD BASIN

OH-BE-JOYFUL

SKELETON MESA

THE DANCE OF
YELLOW LIGHTNING
OVER THE RIDGE

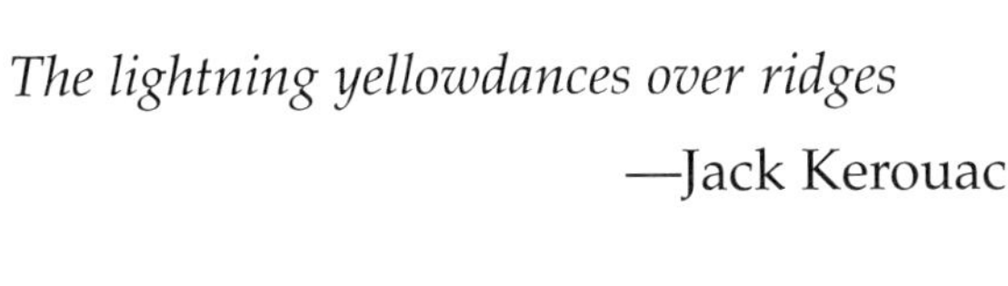

The lightning yellowdances over ridges
—Jack Kerouac

To *You*

Poet of the Future

Balanced Rock

UTE PASS

In my granite dreams
    I listen for the voice
of snow buttercups
  at the edge of retreating drifts.

In my dolomite dreams
I fear not Oblivion's steep narrows
     where hailstones kiss
in the fingers of grass.

In mica dreams
a primrose blooms
    where dead pines rot—
Remember the bones & be not dismayed.

In my quartz dreams
I say only this—
  the crystal earth is covered
     with rainbows.

17 August 1993

BROKEN RIVER

after Neruda

The orange light
of wheatfields
is read by the sun.
Agate and carnelian
replace sap & wood.
The emerald with its green flame
passes on to another.
On his loom, the moss weaver
fills your dead heart with stones.
Time runs like a broken river
across the blue skeleton
of my homeland.
To harden the earth
the rocks took charge.

17 October 1993

WORLD GRIEF

No difference, your grief and the world's.
The weaponless, the broken, the unborn's grief.
From the Colorado River to the Tibetan Plateau.
Not one is spared, all carry world grief.
She at the Lost Highway's Last Off-Ramp.
He of Visions dimmed by infernal mortality.
Even you who feels not herself, himself, at risk.
You whose spirit is the promise of Wilds.
A warmaker's prayer never answered in full.
Gold-lipped diplomats, gold speeches, gold tombs.
You who see sickness as a red badge of courage.
Those who convert to join the dying & dead.
You, spontaneous, open-hearted, being peace.
Someone, everywhere, touching world grief.

11 December 1993

WU XIAONAI

In August 1942, a Japanese plane circled low over rice paddies surrounding Congshan, China. The rats of the village started to die en masse within two weeks. Then fever struck, killing 392 out of 1,200 residents.

Wu Xiaonai was only 18 when the fever seized her. She made the mistake of walking to the Buddhist temple because the Japanese doctors there had posted signs that they could treat the deadly bacteria that formed the basis of their biological warfare.

But it had been a trap. An old woman told of hearing Wu Xiaonai pleading for her life to the doctors as they tied her to a chair and placed a hood over her head to muffle her screams. Then they dissected her to remove her organs for study.

January 1994,
Addendum:
January 1997

VIEWING *SHINDLER'S LIST* ON MARTIN LUTHER KING DAY, 1994

the eyewitness passes.

in the nightclubs of survival
a thousand souls
weep.
        what's moving inside you?
who's the changer
                who changed you?
stolen elections.
        stolen powers.
the smell of unfinished wood around
        windows.
                    what if neil armstrong
had planted a swastika on the moon?

        no more
        auction block
        no more
        salt.

they shall know you
because ghosts will tell them
                        in nightmares
& bloodied dictators
                with broken necks
on sudden gallows will point
with woefully
        amputated hands.
                        even grim teeth
            will rise like flowers
from the earth
        to call out your name
in dreams.

17 January 1994

I GIVE UP MY PLACE IN THE WORLD TO COME

I give up my place in the world to come.
You go instead, it's yours. Let me remain
here, alongside cancer children in orange wigs,
with children in the ground, cruel bullets
like pressed flowers in their smiling faces. Don't
wait for me. Don't wait up, women & men, torn
from each other's side. Whole cities & nations.
The light beyond, like omniscience in the novel.
Give me the ever present exodus, the exodus, the
fire-in-the-tree-of-Life-&-Death-that-does-not-burn
exodus of people living in the impeccable alley of
centuries. Give me huge drowning floods & bitterest
cold. I give up my place. Leave me in this gruesome
factory to glow & hiss & rot. Dress me in the silent
clothes of the terrorized in their poor houses
crushed beneath the homeless blue stones of war.
Persecute me for my starving wall of violets. Lock
me up with the unpenitent in the braided garlic
jails of birth. Just cross out my name when the
saints last call. Send the one who bleeds to death
with apples falling on the dark street. Order those
dragged by snipers across the teacups of explosives
& the undertow of oceans first. Until devoured
like the others in the ovens of churches & pits &
stadiums & caves, I give you my place
to prepare your reward of springtimes,
of innocence, of romance & murder.

31 January 1994

THE LOST CITY OF FEBRUARY

In the monogamy of uncertainty
Anger smells like the handles
Of a burnt coffee pot.
                              Invisibles,
I hear your stealth jukebox
Perseverating with secrets—secret
Names like tiny snowmen
                              climbing up
Charlie Parker in Bellevue, 1954.

No attachments, hearts connected,
Tell me about untowardness, being
At a narrow pass exposed to harm.

Springs flow down from the mountains
Of homicide O homicide, Big River,
Always looking back at urns & roses
   & green fire.

5 February 1994

7 GUITARS

Melinda played her big orange Gretsch. There were
crickets outside, but she could not hear them. She was
listening thru the headphones now, listening to the
night, the blues, the volume, the dark.
                              The song was
about a daughter & how her mother, all the way to her
dying, kept silent & hidden & scrubbed the floors—her
daughter pinned against floors, pinned to floors.
                              Melinda
rips thru her solo on the big orange Gretsch, taking
the words to the out-section now. From her hands you
see a girl in a slip her mother gave her special for
the prom—
                    a girl with the penis of her father in her
mouth on prom night. On the fifth take, Melinda bends
each note so hard you feel Time falling thru clotheslines
of torn dresses, falling
                              & still falling—dead mothers
like archangels falling through the mouths of daughters
pinned beneath sinks. Calmly, she brushes back her
platinum hair.
                    No one in the control room can see that
she unhooks her strap, takes off her fingerpicks,
slips the Gretsch into its case.
                              The fog of early
morning covers the lemon trees, the blossoming
acacias, the horses, the moss-covered oaks. She
wraps the red scarf around her neck—
                              the scarf from
a drummer she met in Prague. Melinda stacks her 7 guitars
she brought to the session in the back of her van. In the
dawn air she dreams of the light that lights the light.

                                        18 February 1994

CHISOS MOUNTAINS

- 11 -

Half moon in the fading light,
Green through the Window,
Dark-green, the desert floor.

Under the spell of rock, cloud,
Smoky quartz, wind—

All that is never seen, but once.

Traveling with blue jays up pinnacles,
Casa Grande above us still.

There, a spotted white-tailed doe
In the twilight grass, evergreen sumac,
Oak leaves & juniper, sotol, lechuguilla,
Prickly pear, mesquite bean.

Night now, a large ring around the moon.
Its hue the yellow of summers lost.

21 March 1994

MOUNTAINS UPON MOUNTAINS

Two small daisies beneath a fern.
The faces of rock—smooth, orange & petrified.
A taste of rain on the lips of thorns.

Trees hanging from cliffs.
Hundreds of juniper overhanging cliffs.

All the people of the world hanging on
Like trees—half living, half dead.
Questioned by stones.
Stained by the rose moon.

Red barrel cactus blossoms here.
Mexico just beyond the river.

Mountains upon mountains
Upon mountains.

Tiny acorns in cool nameless shadows.

22 March 1994

CACTUS PRAYER AT MULE EAR'S PEAK

- 13 -

under the
juniper berry
sky, the path's
so close,
somewhere
between you
& these hands
which balance
the green eyes
of death
that come
out of the earth
to devour us.

23 March 1994

SIERRA DEL CABALLO MUERTO TO THE RIO GRANDE

Lying on the Marufa Vega trail
in a blue arroyo, on cool stones—
air still hot from the day.
Wind at the pass. Rio Grande below.

Thunder & rain, middle of the night.
Paintbrush in the canyons, burros & wild dogs.
Butterflies washing the dust from their wings.

At the river, with her white moths,
bank swallows, weeping dragonflies,
The galloping of dead horses.
The silence of clouds.

If I'd known such a river awaited,
I'd have gone down long ago.

24 March 1994

MOUNTAIN LION MEDITATION

deep
in the canyons
of south boulder creek
the secret
of every life
awakens in silence.

the pasque flower blooms
in the middle of me
near a set
of fresh tracks
where snows first
withdrew.

18 April 1994

The Long House Of Bardos

NEW VERSION TO OLD SPIRITUAL

swing low
  sweet emptiness
coming to
  enlighten me.
heat in
  the valley,
moonlit
  high peaks
still covered
  with snow—
swing low
  sweet love
so blind,
  coming for to
weave me
  into joy's beautiful
darkness,
  where the
angels film
  the chase
scenes for
  their action movies.

26 April 1994

WITH THE EARTH WHEN SHE DIED
IN MY FLYING DREAM

Last night I dreamt the earth died after millennia traveling
in her old shoes. With her as she takes her last breath,
I close her eyes,

Watch as her lips blow last song & all gentle natures ascend.
I bathe the dusty feet, the giving hands entwine.
Prepare the husk—

My planet's bones. Wrap the shroud with its jackals
& bluebirds & refugees & cities where there was
CNN, but no food.

From balanced rock, thru tip of clouds & golden light, I
earth's coffin lower into the Void, over people
by dead people

Divided & hearts like grass beneath snow-covered pine.
Over ribs & one-handed mariachis & children's books
I gaze once more

At her redwoods & canyons of deep fire & avalanches
of grey-blue silence. Then, with shooting stars, I fill
her unmarked grave.

2 May 1994

SOUTH MESA

the night
feels so different
                    riding with my brother
in the cool open air

ducks overhead
            new colts & calves

in the fields
            near marshall.

                        yellow stars
chase us down

chrome red canyons
of the midnight moon.

we stop at south mesa
walk to the bridge,

not saying much, looking
            into one another's eyes,

looking away.
it all feels so new—

the roads & wind
the hands of granite

reaching out to
touch the sky.

13 May 1994

WEIRD ASS

What a weird ass karma—going backwards,
     lost tenses, the serial present, nothing past.
Boys on supermarket floors devouring comic books in the
     blue vagina light of ATMs.
Scarlet armpit-hair dyejob girls burning telephones
     with their gothic eyes.
The gigantic & fugitive masculine thirst neither presence
     nor shadow, by no fingers or light captured.
Weird ass Buddhas in North Dakota sitting in the arched
     willow sweatlodge emptiness of the soul.
Weird ass electro strawberry magnetic fields forever
     crashing down a coitus of stairwells into
               the vain kitchenette where one is giving up
& one is holding up a dawn of shining yellow flowers.

                              18 May 1994

WHEN ROBOTS CRY

When robots cry, do they call up their friends
      & go out for milkshakes?
Is it for all the inventions never invented?
Is it for New York City? Hong Kong? Atlantis? Mars?
Are they burned out on automation?
Sick of guiding missiles, guiding bombs, guiding weapons,
      guiding Death?
Is it the body parts of children sticking out of the ground
      that makes them cry?
Is it because nobody sees a robot shooting up electricity
      as having a problem?

10 June 1994

IN THE LONG HOUSE OF BARDOS

Mandala of sunflowers. Stars
Peyote stitched across the night.
All the things we never said.
That later we must give away.
Rocks floating in the air. The
Small rainbow beneath a rose.
Now she burns as well as I. Time
Runs out, but love grows true.

4 July 1994

NOTES FROM A TRIBUTE TO ALLEN GINSBERG
BY SHARON OLDS

She places a shoebox on the table, undoing the string, & says she remembers the City Lights edition of *Howl* was small enough to keep under her clothes. She spoke about the line, his use of the long line, & how talking was not permitted by her family during dinner.

String isn't used much in this way anymore. It was the kind of string kept for years and for which we one day find our heart's bursting, the things inside scattering out, almost forcing us to return. This was the string she undid as she spoke of poetry introducing itself to her.

She takes the lid off the shoebox, carefully lifting out a white mask she had made of her face as a child. She lifts it out as if she were someone removing from a big storefront window a tiny white card that reads "closed for mourning." Tying the mask behind her head, she says that whatever is written upon the forehead of a mask, these are the words written in that person's heart.

She sits a moment in silence, in memory of the person of the mask on her face, and the words she had placed upon the forehead of the mask, words she had written when she wore that face, were from "Supermarket in California," a poem he had written about the hunger of love that reaches beyond the grave & the nectar of speech & unknowingly, a girl—

What America did you have when Charon quit poling his ferry and you stood watching the boat disappear on the black waters of Lethe were the words she had painted upon the forehead of the mask of the girl she had been at the table. It was the long line of his poems placed against her skin that made him, she said, the first person she let be her.

8 July 1994

ELECTION DAY NEWS FROM
SAN MARTIN DE LAS PIRAMIDES

The heart of polling place 4115, District 21
is this sturdy wooden table covered with a
                         hand-embroidered cloth.
Casting the first vote, the old farmer
emerges from behind the white plastic curtain,
his thumb marked with indelible ink.

Outside the butcher skins a cow.
Blue-headed turkeys peck the hard dirt.
A family of four makes tire patches all day
        in the shadows of pyramids at Teotihuacan.

                         25 August 1994

THE STONES FROM UP ON WHEELCHAIR ROW

Moon & stars over Mile High Stadium
As the Rolling Stones open their
Voodoo Lounge Tour Denver show with
"Not Fade Away" & the sparks are
Flying on wheelchair row—the dead
Leg'd boys waving their arms, clapping
Gloved hands, chanting each word of
"Satisfaction," weeping during "Miss
You" for the long gone souls of the
Departed. It's a transistor radio
8-track night & we're laughing when
The black-booted girl in the short
Silk dress dances between these men,
Sits on their laps, wonders if they
Feel a thing—grins with a cat-eyed
Smile as the music shifts into "Street
Fighting Man," & how deeply her long
Tongue sinks into the mouths of the
Love strong boys on iron-wheel alley.

15 September 1994

The Place No One Knew

MY LOVE, YOU ARE LIKE GLEN CANYON

You are all that is wet.
All that is slickrock.
Arches, towers, palisade.
All that is kindness.

All that 10 million years
Of erosion have cut into
Plateaus, laccolithic domes.
All that touches badlands.

Ancestral paradox formations.
All the orange globe mallow.
White moon in the western sky.
All that catches stardust.

You are the salt valley.
All that's Navajo sandstone.
That's like Glen Canyon—
"The place no one knew."

23 September 1994

THINGS TO PUT IN YOUR COFFIN

Tire iron.
Flashlight.
Steinway concert grand piano.
Divorce papers.
A bong.
Night-vision goggles.
Gatorade for zombies.
The light green air pollution of January.
An elephant on stilts walking across the ocean.
Frankincense & mammograms.
Sunglasses.
Coffee-maker.
Cessna wing nut off single engine plane Frank Eugene Corder
      crashed into the White House.
The Mayflower Compact.
Styrofoam peanuts.
"Letter from Birmingham Jail."
Farmer's hoe.
Lipstick.
A movie set from *The Ten Commandments*.
Book of stamps.
Cellular phone.
Interior murals of wagon trains.
Answering machine for all the dead children
      trying to reach you.

24 September 1994

ELK SCRAPED ASPEN BARK

Walking quietly thru lodgepole woods.
Past elk scraped aspen bark.
Western mountains covered with snow.
Yesterday's thunder a memory.

In shadow, a tall blue spruce—
Its silent needles pierce the hail.
More stars than purple juniper berries.
Old roots exposed to rain & snow.

The yucca shakes its rattle clear.
Mist at dusk—the green breath of wandering elk.
In the velvet autumn light
I smell the hay stuck to your sweater.

2 October 1994

IT IS SAID THAT INTELLECTUALS FROM THE UNIVERSITIES WROTE LISTS OF THOSE TO BE SLAUGHTERED

A grave with 1,400 bodies uncovered.
Four thousand more found at Gafunzo

       near the border with Zaire.
At Mabanza, mass graves containing more than 7,000.
1,000 refugees buried outside the Ndera Psychiatric Center
    in a small forest.

Almost all the 750 mentally handicapped patients
   fired upon with bullets & grenades—
     milling aimlessly,
        eight miles from Kigali,
       singing with their hands in the air.

        6-10 October 1994

CLOUDS DESCEND LIKE SPACESHIPS FROM NIRVANA

Pumpkins sit at their typewriters crazed.
Redwing blackbirds swallow the sky.
Longs Peak changes out of his smoky clothes.
Meadowlarks sing in the yellow dusk.
Two white herons in a pond so still.
Cool green mist off front range hangs.
Sunflowers think they are invincible.
Ants remember how the earth was made.

16 October 1994

HUNGER FALLING ALL AROUND

for Gary Allen

Hunger gathered   upon the earth
chanted the   names of all the
mountains   & rats & corn
& green   snowflakes in the
late afternoon   box canyon light.
You fell   thru an opening
in the rock   breathlessly towed
underground   thru 84,000 vaginas
of dark hunger   falling into the sea
like a ghost   wandering shadowland,
his eyes   a diamond ocean lunchpail
hunger   like skull furniture
vowel   wicked candles
in the sugary   cinnamon roll
emptiness   where ancestors
practice star   names given by
the yellow   dance of
lightning   over the ridge

28 October 1994

ENTERING THE DARK TIME

we won't see
the yellow shoe
of days
on the androgynous
burgundy
sweepstake turnip
home cave
magpie
shakedown—
only our
dead lovers' horses
riding
backwards
through the sea
of bluebirds
& comas & apples
& goddess angel
saint merrymakers
thirsting at the
waterfall of
mulberry
imcomprehensibilities
where
the poor
man who cloaks himself
bares his
heart to you.

2 November 1994

NAKED GURU KIVA MOSH PIT

after Whitman

Naked guru kiva mosh pit, while I was dreaming,
    you were the one moving the world.

You are the endless settlements of indifferent demons
    making out on the sofa

Of green bone town centuries—maiming the maimed,
    the Maiming of the Maimed.

A sound like a cricket, a sound of doors weeping
    between two underworlds

That I may fill my hymns to the earth, that you
    may rise in the morning & find a

Heart to call upon, waiting to make joyous hymns
    to the whole planet's inner beauty,

Hymns that would see through the frivolous Judge,
    corrupt Governor, the dicta of officers

& Congressmen, their forgotten pain coiled in the blood-
    soaked bluebells of democratic elections.

The way it was separate, inseparable. The way it is
    a naked guru kiva mosh pit

Anticipating the chemotherapies of emotional horror
    all pressed close, gasping, wild-eyed.

8 November 1994

JEMEZ MOUNTAINS MEDITATION

The brown scrub oak leaf
    splits a boulder like an axe.
Pine needle flattens widest rock.
A snowflake pocks the hardest stone.
The blue juniper berry crumbles
    whole mountains into shards.
An ant's footsteps carve out
    riverbeds without end.
One raindrop sharpens a peak's
    dull edge.
Stardust explodes a canyon wall.
The weight of rainbows holds
    continents in place.

25 November 1994

AIRFONE

after Wang Wei

Ten video screens above the aisle.
Johnny Carson reruns on each one.
I close my eyes, dream of redwoods—
The Chilula believed redwoods divine
    beings.
The Ohlone considered redwoods the
    most intelligent of all trees.
The flight attendants look so withered
    beneath the 10-screened dancing girl.
Passing thru white clouds I flash
    on the earth—
Filled with bones till the end
    of time.

Denver to San Francisco
20 December 1994

LIKE WANG WEI IN THE CHUNGNAN FOOTHILLS

Like Wang Wei in the Chungnan foothills
So many are the sights I alone must know.
The smooth sumac bent around this boulder.
Its dried red berry music rattling the wind.
Winter stars curve along the half moon's path.
Sheer cliff echo of crooked stream below.
Tiny snow islands melting afternoon grass.
Ecstatic leaping mule deer up dry riverbed.
Lonely sand-filled skull forgotten by ants.
Mouthless tooth, storybook candy of the soul.
Golden eagle, its pair white diamond wings.
Piece of sun the meadowlark stole.
The hundred miles of leafless cottonwood root.
Vain evening hopes that you would join me.

16 January 1995

Red Buteo'd Heart

CONTRIBUTING TO THE ONE GREAT POEM

I want to contribute to the One Great Poem.
The One Great Poem that is made by all the participants.
All the people alive at this moment.
People that had lived and would live in days ahead.

You, the One Great Poem, I want your lines to include the
        Dalai Lama's theory of National Karmas.
To include nations sane, mobs of coked nations,
Nations deranged, generation after generation ruled by
        secret police.
Here I place those who believed the enemy had no bullets.
That the enemy had no ammunition, that the enemy
        would not shoot back.

I want to stand alongside those of the Automatic Weapons Plague—
        shooting without thinking, shooting without aiming.
Alongside those who walk among bodies covered with plastic sheets.
Among the Sponsors of the Strength & Beauty of All Children Act.
Nobody can filibuster the whole of experience.
With more than a million million watchtower blue-dime stars,
        what thief could filibuster the One Great Poem.

I offer up fresh seafood, white raincoats, Frank O'Hara's
        "At Kamin's Dance Bookshop."
A shoe-lace knot, eyeglasses splattered with blood.
The Weddell Sea, the Beaufort Sea, all the mosques between Gaza
        & the Sunset Strip.
Xian—most renowned of China's six ancient capitals, 100 horses,
        yellow lip-rings, a green pager.
Hidden assumptions of how journalists frame public perception.

Mental slavery, compact laser disc video game boy Data Barons
        & their Museums of On-Line Genocide Delirium Art.
Those who keep scrapbooks of abortion clinic storm troopers,
        White House bombers, the Fugitive President.
Dried grass heaped together & burned on hazy afternoons.
The way deaf people look at leaves.

Radishes & lemons, the blink of neon donut stands.

A boy covered with butterflies floating on green clouds
          enlaced in the trembling brown ink of silence—
When I turn & look in, the One Great Poem goes always
          onward at dusk, past empty nests.
Against the sides of muletail & bluestem, sometimes
          crouched low like a coyote in the east.
Like a rising moon that follows the crystal lit grotto'd
          sweatlodge of night.

Troubled planets, laid off, sitting numb in Television
          Universe—you contribute here.
How many Milky Ways left on drawing boards undone.
Crumbling rings, junkyards of galaxies compacted.
Homeless black holes with lesions purplish & cruel.
Eternity unshaven, old newspapers in his coat, mumbling
          in Astral Gutter.
All the Passing Through passing through the passing
          through of the One Great Poem.

Not an Infomercial about the thighs of big government, the
          liposuction of the Common Good.
Not about Virtual America, Democratic Euthanasia Vistas.
What purpose technologic appliance if only to speed-fax anger,
          to digitalize rage?
No tumors upon humanity, frogs, swarms of flies, murrain upon
          cattle, locusts upon the barley & flax in bloom.
No Oswiecim where So Many left behind only the smell of their
          burning bodies—
A wanderer among you, the One Great Poem will never cease.
How sweet the flesh that touches the sacred, the same sacred
          I also touched.

You who reported of elves, of Autocrats buried in quicksand,
          buried with clay armies—
The stones in the river they are myself, the magician
          with talking severed head on a plate.
The World's Largest Office Party, the little home for a
          caterpillar in a cassette case.
The music pushing itself back into the crimson piano.
Gregory Corso's lost manuscript *Who Am I—Who I Am*, stolen
          from Chelsea Hotel, 1974.
A gnashing of states drowned, where no one hears the sobbing.
Nor the burning of the Wheel of Fire, the One Great Poem.
Nothing ever is or can be lost nor ever die.

The Great Poem joins you on snowfield at treeline, joins
          you barefoot along secluded riverbank edge.
Corner of all that shows & all that shows not—a dogwood's
          shadow, cardinal in the oaks, Paris in April.
A crisis job interview, alone in almond orchard chewing grape
          bubble gum in the rain at dawn.
Women without breasts, golden cities of tomorrow.
Any limited judgment of the realness of the feeling of Self,
          the Selfness of others.
All that is non-existent, joined by the One Great Poem.

And what if writing suddenly appears on the sun, would it
          say you are always traveling—
You who wanted to feel the world from outside Paradise,
          yet higher than ruins & pyramids.
Higher than all the Floods, all the Ys ever spoken
          piled on top of one another.
Higher than all the songs of each extinct animal note for note.
Than a billion World Trade Centers stacked on end,
          than Monolithic State & Monolithic Gods.
Than the Doors of Night where the prophets break in,
          "Truth scored on their palms."

Great Poem, you are a raven, a name spelled backwards,
          a clock with no face.
You are all that is underneath the earth, the burning magma furnace
          Core that greases Time's gears.
Your year's like an angel flying through a steel wall
          heavy with violets & antelope & rootbeer.
Your stanzas weep like crickets on lightning bolts in joy's
          ruby-bone-box painted skeleton heart.

One Great Poem, when I turn & look in I see grey wolves
          moving South.
Ash remains in spring ponds, drinking fountains, lunch counters bare.
Island of Stone, four chords of thunder, Wise Neanderthal mother &
          father on forced Hunger Strike.
A one-armed poolshark chalking his cue.
When I turn & look in I see the sad beautiful radios of linen rooms &
          mail rooms & laundry rooms & boiler rooms.
That is how I found out I was exactly like you &
          everybody else.

How much longer before you attempt the dreams of your heart?
As you wait for Liberation, report on it—surrounded by bodyguards,
          holding a blown-up satellite phone.
You, on Very Dangerous Street, Very Dangerous Bridge,
          you on Very Dangerous City Square.
With a tag on your smooth tiny wrist among fallen electricity wires,
          ruptured pipelines spewing gas.
As you Spook the public, as you Veto the peace, as you sweep up
          around an automobile riddled with holes.
As you detonate yourself to Kingdom Come, as they scrape your flesh
          off the boulevard.

As a child fills herself with watermelon seeds, thinking she'll
          grow watermelon vines inside her.
As a small boy wonders what it's like to be a male ladybug.
Each is filled with the One Great Poem, slim & graceful as a deer
          in the nakedness of the land.
In the nakedness of Taskmasters' mortar & straw.
Naked with the story of Water, the naked bitterness of water,
          bitter water we cannot drink.
The sweet Naked kiss of Water against your lips.

When you feel what dies within dying & you let it die
          this too is the One Great Poem.
When you feel the Wind that shattered the rocks around
          Elijah's cave & Milarepa's cave.
In your Revelation, as you lift back the Veils, especially
          those who have given up their Quest.
Those who emerge with no answer at all, defeated by
          storms without end.
Wondering if the Always Being Born & Everywhere
          really exists.
Married to Emptiness, this too, who you are is hiding there.

Between the orange solitudes of lineage & the jasmine solitudes
          of burial move on, take the name you give yourself.
Even & upright, the Mind abides nowhere, in a quiet series
          of haiku, in future scrolls.
With them on the Ship of Cyberfools.
& they who with cybersorrow drift the cyberstreets.

                                        23 January 1995

TO ONE I SAW DESPONDENT AT A RAVE

after Frank O'Hara

Reach into my blue refrigerator,
The one filled with purple clocks of night
& bedspreads the color of ammonia.

Phone numbers change, still people call.
The yellow chair kisses the floor.
The sky is a factory, leaning—

Leaning, almost touching the ground.
All I can do is promise my tears
They are not a shining moon.

An orange room knows no sorrow
& the moon shining in a cold spring
is not the moon. The moon is

Where it always is, in the bottomless
Chasm of your blue eyebrows—
This is the way the living must fare.

20 February 1995

ON ROOFTOP, DENVER PRESS CLUB, THINKING ABOUT CASSADY

for Jack Collom

Tree & Ken & Jack & I were driving Highway 36, trying to get to the
Denver Press Club by 7:00 for Jack to be on the panel of writers who
could be the next poet laureate of Colorado, past the new Elitch amuse-
ment park down in the trainyard flats, the hypnotic ferris wheel lights
spiraling in the darkness, down Colfax all the while talking about
recording studios & medieval poet laureates & Jack's famous butter &
tabasco sandwiches, Sue Rhynhart, Tree's dream about Newt Gingrich.
Richard & Holly were at the Press Club selling books, & Michelle was
there. The bar downstairs was packed with suits—a rack of ties knotted
at the bottom of the steps. I imagine big cigars, hats pushed back on
cub reporters' heads, ancient ebony chipped rotary phones & scream-
ing editors, headstrong gorgeous curly-haired Pulitzer Prize winners
slapping some sense into a cold blooded braindead copyboy lost on
his beat, but all I saw as we passed through was some dropsy-eyed
blonde in a green velour dress whining about Pueblo to a drunk jew-
elry salesman without a clue. The laureate panel was half beauty
pageant, half ethereal caucus with pleas & rants of enduring values
& how the mountains are not blue nor us, how "we are biodegradable,"
even our "pothole sonnets." From the rooftop where I went at intermis-
sion I could see the Brown Palace, yucca & rattlers with their eyes like
Cha-Cha's black pearls, the ones she'd saved up for a long time. It was
a warm February night. The ice-caps must be melting, seas rising, not
near enough money to keep the Titanic of sinking countries afloat.
Wonder what Neal Cassady was doing right now this moment his
high-speed Denver Larimer poolhall Youth—Jack Collom sitting with
long blue heron neck sagacious mustache tender windswept face,
brain full of gold rush UFO pony express cattle skull near poison pool

high plain stagecoach wagon train pulled by eight pink cadillacs down
sage brush arroyos where people had no glimmer of vast cities to come,
millions of buffalo stampeding at the choke of midnight, mud on the
slip of Dancehall Belle in Salmon, Idaho—those were the days! And
then there's speeches addressed to the governor, cake with enormous
orange candles that melt on the icing to go with the bourbon & people
are coming over to say things like "Your cowboy boots are outhouse uri-
nals of jailbreaks in eternity" & "Colorado—with her white mountain
heather & palominos, crazyweed, lupine, sweetvetch & steer's
head—comes to you like a god shooting ten arrows of pure love into
your red buteo'd heart" & Jack's in the car now with his Mexican walk-
ing stick & dead left hand, pulling that tabasco & butter sandwich out of
old plastic baggy recycled perhaps since his days in the '40s at A&M
while we're talking about Reed's dissertation, Larry's visit last week,
Teachers & Writers, getting tickets to see Willie Nelson at the Grizzly
Rose, high school wrestling, Peter Orlovsky staying in dingy 28th Street
motel row room, yelling at 7-Eleven sales lady for not giving him a bag
for picnic supplies as anyone will do in New York City, even if you're
just buying a peanut, & Tom having to smooth things out before they
all go joyriding up Flagstaff, & then, under Pine Street lamplight Jack
is "writing in his notebook" (his palm) something before going inside &
me I'm curious about Julius & Lafcadio, worried about Andy Clausen in
Oakland with herniated disk—how will he carry the trillions of bricks
up wheelbarrow life flat on his back—so, you tell me, what's the differ-
ence between what's good & what happens?

25 February 1995

TREVOR'S KOAN

for Andy Clausen

How do you know it's
      Enlightenment—does it finish
Your sentence? Is it painted
      On a U.N. wall?
          What part dies?
          Which part gives?
      What part is lost?
What part lives?

What was your alibi?
      Can you hurt others
Without the hurt
      Hurting you? Will
         It cut the
         Deficit?
      Do you still
Feel separate—

Hypnotized by joy?
      How do you see it?
What does it change?
      Can politics kill it?
         Can anyone really
         Take it away?
      If it's enlightenment
What stays?

26 February 1995

MUSEX

To those who believe they're beyond
The interdependence of all beings, I send
You this memo cc'd MusEx.

With MusEx delivery I liberate the World Bank,
The Fortune 500, Tokyo Foreign Exchange,
Cali Cartel, Russian Plutonium Mafia,
Warlords & Slumlords, Underworld Leaders,
Crime Boss Arms dealers, Black Marketeers,
Launderers upon launderers, White Collar Thieves,
TV Execs with their bleak gothic visuals,
Oil Reserve Magnets, Billionaire Candidates
Buying seats in the legislature, purchasing votes.

Hitmen, hackers, henchmen & heathens,
Fasting ex-presidents, Shepherds of a False Divine,
Body Lobbyists, Distribution Kings,
Talk-radio cons, Soap Opera Queens,
Skinheads & bookies & Phony Wise Users
Decommissioning wilderness into tiny green
Museum hatboxes stuffed with cash,
Real estate agent of the silicon chip,
The silicon implant, the silicon mind,
Globe market junkies, Infoslut barons
Franchising children with microwave skies,
Big Wheels riding from nowhere to nowhere
In the luxurious & melanin comforts of greed's decay—
Each could live simply, without attachments,
Without the craving of Arrogant Mind.

So fast is my carrier, even Light's engine blows
& crumples upon other lost planets filled with
Violent desks & the madnesses of office furniture
& calculators & the general wailing of the nameless
Streets where broken hearted Economies go.

6 March 1995

TEEN FAITH

after Jacques Prévert

Sometimes I'm overwhelmed by the future.
I don't know how I'll get there.
I'm afraid I'll shut out shut down shut off.
Because I'm alone, there must be something
   wrong with me.

Time passes so quickly in geometry class.
I'm writing you a book so huge
Each letter will take a gallon of paint.
The pages float around my mind
   like ropewalkers dancing on stilts.

If you heart's slowly breaking
Remember "The Dunce" who with chalk of every color
"On the blackboard of misfortune
Draws the face of happiness."

8 March 1995

PETER ORLOVSKY'S JACK KEROUAC LECTURE & REVELATION: PENNY LANE, 13 MARCH 1995

Giant shaving cut under nose, rosary, fat tie,
sport jacket, thick head of silver hair like Boris
Yeltsin battling totalitarian Forest Services of
Polka Dot ambulance drivers in happy garbage can
lid loneliness, smiling in blue, white & red stamp
machine cafe static black noise ringing through
the mortuary silences of toothless, ragged America.
Peter Orlovsky putting out his smoke with
tennis shoe bottom, says, "I have very good news,
important news for everyone. Stop talking. Turn
your two eyes into ears. Turn the kettle off. Turn
the camera off. I don't want you to repeat this.
Listen. Forget about what I'm going to tell you.
If you write it down you're in for a lot of trouble.
Don't even talk to a tree about it. Shhhhhhhh.
I found out that Kerouac was reborn. In the Bronx.
He's 25 years old. Kerouac has come back. He's got
a very cranky mother in the Bronx. We spent the
day together. I'll repeat it for the last time.
Kerouac is back. He's much more healthy and strong.
And he's working very hard. Doesn't have much time
to write. He has 4 brothers. Maybe three brothers
and a sister. He writes mostly in his heart—
heart poetry. That's about it. I never said nothing.
It's a secret, and it can't leave this room."

CAN'T BLAME THE PAST FOR YOUR OWN DEATHWISH

for Rebeckah Medina

i wish there was something
to show, others showed me
what i always thought a
door, miserable, i never
would've found you, honest,
never thought it'd stop,
the you know i know you
knew about poverty impov-
erishment, of words &
lover, tho i could boast,
survived, what victory
to be with you, her, is
this rome, i'm human, how
special you are, you don't
even spell my name right,
doesn't matter, i am
entirely aware
he's bigger than orange flames
shooting thru windows,
her house, made of leaves
& poolhalls, green apples &
hearts hanging from the
sky, shape of mountains,
lab books filled with
chemistry, brain tumors
from too much deathwishing,
not enough letters to the
nation, not enough letters
written—change the world,
change the worlds that
empty themselves thru your
breath at night in the rain
when the forsythia blossom &
your face covers the wind.

18 March 1995

TRUST

I'll write about it for a few minutes.
What's that called when they squeeze the air
out of a needle? When your hawk flies low?
Rust will help me move like a horse in a
winterfield shifting the weight from one leg
to the other. Talk to me—that rapist, she
said she loves him. Anne Frank, she loved
them from behind her hidden book case. If
we had white pens could we write on your
black dress about spelling errors in subtitles
of foreign films? A Bosendorfer piano made of
Leggos. Waiting room TV shows brutal stabbings
while on gurneys dead bodies pass, passing
the funerals & weddings called off. The doesn't
that doesn't come. What they don't tell you
about yin & yang & elk slow moving in a
blizzard, Ella Fitzgerald's legs, bears coming
out of stars, hundred year old pines, what
death is like for people with autism, what
Dante knew when speechless intellect sunk
into the abyss more deep than brain cancer—
it eats through paranoia like M.S. does myelin.

1 April 1995

BORDERS BOOKS

after Robert Desnos

I could've been reading on a streetcorner anywhere.
Begging at an exit ramp, broke down at a toll booth gate.
Could of been selling encyclopedias to a rattlesnake,
          life insurance in a morgue
As I looked out on the audience that wasn't there.
I cannot describe the chance performance I gave that night.

My audience was not made up of people I could see
Nor was I reading simply to the non-existing audience
          separate from the audience that wasn't there.
Nothing from my books had power over them—
Not that I had ever lost the devouring love to write.
A million words—nothing could pull us apart.

Mortality's blue shroud was not distracting.
Looking beyond, where the ones I love do not answer,
          You saw me naked among walking dead mummies
And nobody stood aching on the steps of an erroneous vacuum.
Nobody wants to be remembered for anything else
          on this tortured earth except love.

13 April 1995

SWM

Knows how to operate a zipper. You like
Rumi, kisses in blizzards. Is this line secure?
Do you have to tell me you're putting on your
stockings now, putting on your bra? There's
a light & you see it at the end of every mis-
understanding. You see it whether you're with
me or not. In your powerbook are images of
John Wesley Powell's 1871 expedition, the
Sadhana of Mahamudra, children's toys of India,
ex-boyfriend letter telling him to fuck off,
everything ever written by Bernadette Mayer.
I think, how lovely a garden in the clouds
would be. You're wearing dark green lipstick
to the dance tonight. Does your guest registry
include a man who sells UFO abduction plans?
Have you listened to falsity so long you
cannot distinguish the truth within? What
does that Media Kit actually include? Who
does your printing? Where can I get those
fonts? If you shave your legs, do you do a
good job? Is there an entry in your journal
with golden deer kneeling as you pass the
hyacinths, cervical caps, onion rings, plums,
a beehive of hearts cut out from red paper
folded in two, hairspray, garter belts, jade
labyrinth made of alphabets curling inside the
walls of a hundred thousand year old pumpkin?
What's the first half-hour of heaven compared
with you, your dress like a scarlet-painted
maple in October! The marriage of true
minds is all I sought, else human beings have
never loved, nor you sewn the huge rondure
hems of angels' wings—you who make love
so beautifully, your eyes like parks where
Time stands still.

20 April 1995

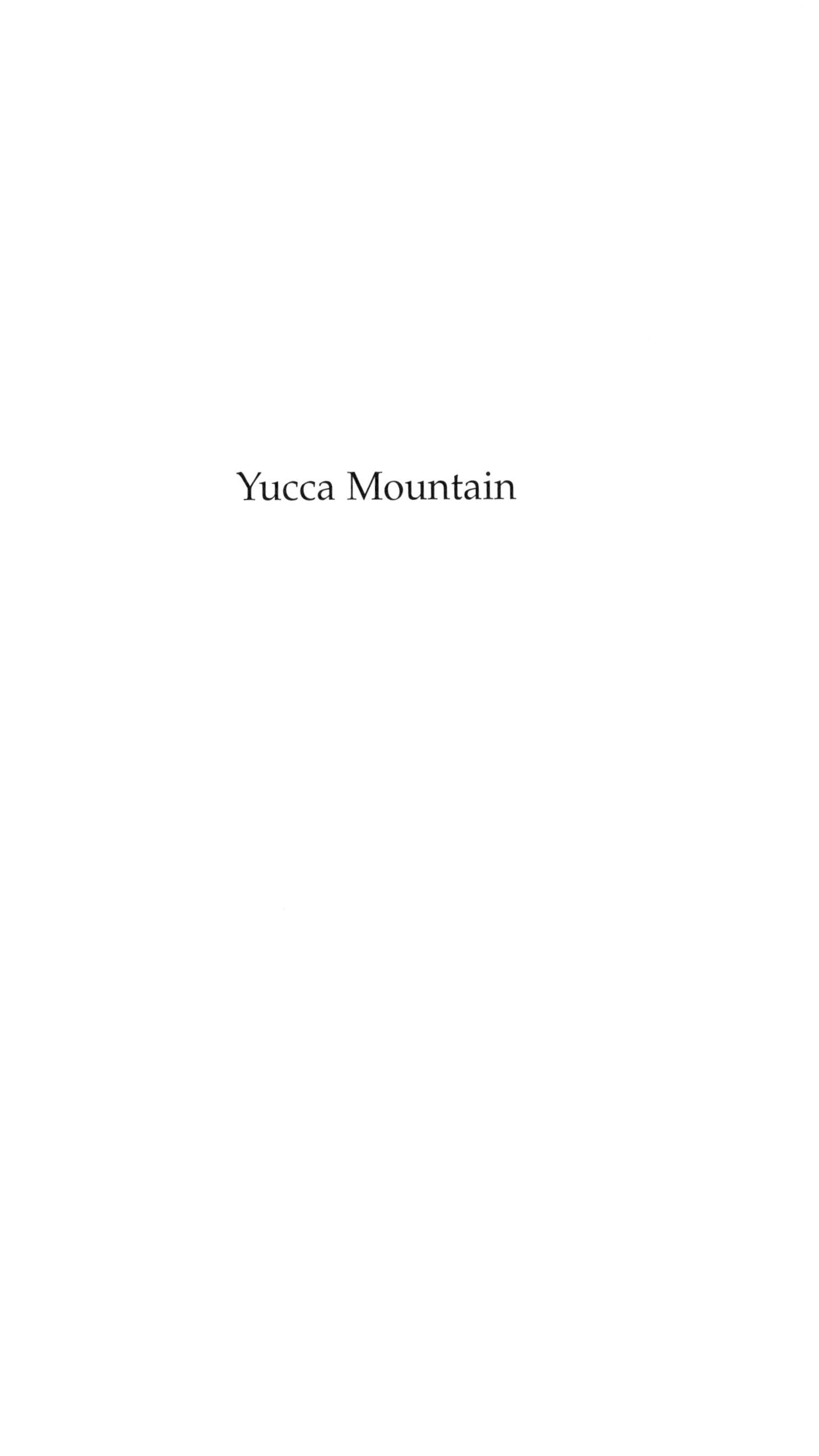

Yucca Mountain

SPELL TO PREVENT NUCLEAR WASTE STORAGE
AT YUCCA MOUNTAIN

This is for you
Yucca Mountain.
We do not want
The ground disturbed.
You are part of the
Whole desert,
Connected by trails
& remembered in
The old songs.

Let there be no end
To your fall rabbit drives.
No end to your
Wild grain & nut harvests.
May your burial
Rockrings & sweatlodges,
Ceremonial cairns,
Musical stones &
Painted walls endure.

May gold cholla
Tell your story.
May yerba mensa, earthstar,
Wiregrass, matchweed,
Four-winged saltbrush,
Greasewood & snowberry,
Creosote bush,
Gum brush & cane
Tell this story.

The ground, air & water—
It is all the same.

May hawk & coyote,
Chuckwalla, deer, wild burro,
Sheep & turtle
Remain as they are.
Dune Wash, Crater
Flats, Fortymile Canyon,
White Rock Spring,
Ash Meadows & Skull Mountain—
Remain as you are.

May your butterflies
Turn back train loads
Of nuclear waste.
May the secret destiny
Of your tears ascend
Like the steps of lost ones
Suddenly heard.

We lose our way
Yucca Mountain.
We who are insignificant.
We whose days are
Only moments to yours.

April 1995

ORTHODONTIST TREKS IN 80 POUNDS DENTAL TOOLS
TO REMOTE VILLAGE IN NEPAL

Ezra Pound arrested, 50 years ago today.
Television is dying & Sarah Vaughn is dead.
Your teeth are an orchestra playing in
        an aquarium filled with Cherry Coke.
Where were you going in such a rush?
Mangos are so temporary, like roller coasters
        made of cottage cheese.
I see you balancing a tall building on fire
        in your heart
But who believes oxygen when I see you in that skirt
Drifting thru the applauding stars
Like a bathing beauty outlined by knives.

5 May 1995

LOSING RELEVANCE BRINGS A COMMITMENT TO FREEDOM

You'll never be Forrest Gump
      Talking to John Lennon on TV
            & you're not the Dalai Lama
Not the President
      Or Louis Farrakhan.

And the computer is much
      Faster than your brain
            & the media's so addictive
And your mother
      And your father

Left you for the Hereafter
      & one day you ask yourself
            What wisdom carries me—
Does it go back to Dante?
      Do you feel its electricity?

Is it a conspiracy?
      Is it all meant to be?
            Does your rage define
All the beauty
      That you're surrendering?

And maybe your handwriting
      Isn't anywhere on the wall
            But every poem you make
Is flawed like clowns
      Begging in a trance.

You just go on your nerve
      Each day losing relevance
            Till maybe you're the only one
In your generation
      Who understood.

7 May 1995

MEETING THE WORLD WIDE WEB SALESMAN

The World Wide Web salesman said he could sell my
books. He could create a site where people could come in
& browse. I felt strange knowing millions of people could
theoretically read about me on the World Wide Web. I
could make the work appeal to these people, but would
any of them actually stop to see my home-page ad? I
knew what the key was, but how could I become *that*
to millions of Websters surfing transglobe? It would be
like a giant flea market. I would have a booth in the big
old optic-fiber mercado. A booth that you'd enter by
walking through honey-drenched corn fields with polar
bears & juniper & hummingbirds & red dancing shoes
for you to wear. But would it be a landscape you'd visit
or would it be just another way to get my money? And
the salesman kept patting his girlfriend's ass, I mean,
right in front of me. After I left, I heard that she threw
that World Wide Web salesman out. He asked when he
could see her again, but she just wouldn't say.

8 May 1995

THE CRICKETS OVERTAKE ME

Frogs grind voids
Into chains of breath.

Robin on a hollow log.
A billion new leaves.

Mallards in the bank-grass hide.
Rivers flood the bridges

That desert the mind.
Stars midwife wind.

Elbows of sky know
The cruel loneliness

Of this earth as
Goldfinch & blackbird speak

Of the darkening everything
Before the coming rain

That opens the clouds for the magic people
To come into our hearts.

22 May 1995

"MINORITY OF JOYNESS"

after Aaron Hicks

Lavender, lemon balm, mint & sage.
Someone burning a flag on the internet.
The girl with silver hands walks in.
Once, you were a radio made of orchids.

I think of you in the night with a
Green jazz glow on your legs
Outside the cold Pepsi machine of
Thunderstorms all dressed in white.

Continuous like August. Your body
Filled with horses. You were killed by swords
Many times. Still, your ankles
Are like butterflies in Las Vegas.

26 May 1995

GHOST TOWN ETIQUETTE

<pre>
All that water
                    raging out the
mountains
                  thru the canyon
past the orioles
                             willows arched
           heads thrown back
                           underdressed,
copiously pierced
                        &
medicated—
                           a steady stream
        of beggars
                            bearing cups
         limousines

           bearing celebrities
                              mussed-hair girls
starchy droves of sailors
                          bus stations, ports
          workaholics
headed home
                             this fast life
        & wanderers
                       headed
        nowhere
</pre>

1 June 1995

UPON READING DAVID COPE'S "THE RHODODENDRON"

I sit in my urban outhouse, David Cope's poem "The
    Rhododendron" in my hands,

Torn open envelope on weary linoleum floor, the words
    "You take a friend in hand & roar

Down blind road after blind road" entering my head
    when the phone rings &

Still reading, I hop across the carpet ball'n'chained
    by my pants dropped shithouse low,

Not as I would like to be seen, but in my best goofball
    pants-around-socks pose,

In slo-mo, glimpsing the Blackburn *Lorca*, that line
    about "cunts full of lilies."

Look at me now—caught mid-crap in thought, purple
    underwear below like a cactus

That blooms only once, a revelation even to myself,
    gazing at brown socks, crumpled jeans,

Remembering myself long ago asleep in a blanket of tulips,
    a boy of light.

"Who can say what love is?"—how I greet my unknown
    caller,

Aware of the mysterious kinship amongst the hairs on my
    legs laughing at dishes piled high in sink.

                              5 June 1995

THE BOX

It was the end of spring. The flooding was
constant after days of rain. Long had they met
in the dream world, and slowly, over the passing
seasons they had learned to say goodbye through
dreams, tossing and turning in separate cities
separated by farms and rivers and moons. The
deer had come off the mountains and were now
walking down the middle of the road. The box
sat in a basement surrounded by hills and people
walking above the earth. They had come to see
one another as someone the other had always
loved and would always love, and this love
was like entering through a burning door into
a burning garden filled with burning roses.
Their voices trembled as each forgotten memento
was lifted far across the plains and lakes and
stars. Lifted towards the freedom between them.
The greater and greater freedom that had always
been there waiting for them.

14 June 1995

SU TUNG P'O: THE HITS

Without knowing it
The snow had drifted into my room.
It is no greater accomplishment to be
A rich corpse or a poor one.
Jewels of jade & pearl
Put in the mouths of the illustrious
Feed the robbers of their tombs.
                    Spring has come again
And the willow cotton is like snow.
I dream of the ancient poet
Who could not distinguish
The peach, the cherry & the apricot.
As for literature, it is its own reward.
Fortunately fools pay little attention to it.
                    Just a wandering bureaucrat
I have been sent to a spot where
The river enters the sea.
I have heard that here, ten feet deep
In the salt marsh, you can find traces
Of the sand, still cold,
Which bubbled up in Chong Ling Spring
High on the rocky plateau.

17 June 1995

THE SHAMAN OF SPEW

Shaman with iris breath of never-ending wind.
Shaman continents navigating seas.
Nutbrown shaman with the ormolu hair.
Shaman Life in which we burn.
Vulgar soothsayer with tambourine onyx.
Shaman at the unguarded frontier pass, thankful for
                a moment's peace.
Shaman with turnpike knees bailing silent waterfalls
                from your persimmon cheek.
Gallows shaman hanging in the Flossenburg dawn.
Mechanical shaman with your chariot of limes and errors.
Shaman of the Golden Thread, shaman awareness.
Beheaded shaman crammed with eels, spiders, scorpions.
Shaman to the wing'd throne of the temple not for sale.
Rope-bridge shaman to the impossible League of Detectives.
Purification shaman—snow, rain, artemisia, dew, oak,
                juniper.
And in thy mind, Beauty.

                                  June 1995

"WRACK EM UP, JIM"

for Tom Peters

Oreo milkshake, squid, maple syrup, yerba santa—
My love is like the Batmobile stuck inside
            a leopard-skin pool stick case.
Laurel & Hardy with Turkish subtitles, Starfleet
            in flames,
You're kinda cute, watch my jacket willya?
Lightning Hopkins on the jukebox.
Tom Peters in black leather walking naked down
            Pearl.
Sometimes you are a peregrine falcon nesting
            on the roof of the Bank of New York.
You are the Glory that is everywhere
Like a band of lapis lazuli in the red summer wheat
But today, it comes like Ronsard at Yosemite.
Lana Turner is dead. Il Postino only rings
            for the lonely gods unsung.
Judge Sabo, you have no business hearing
            Mumia Abu-Jamal's death row appeal.
Governor Ridge, you should grant a reprieve.

4 July 1995

Deluge Shelter

MATANUSKA PRAYER TO DONNA ON HER WEDDING DAY

Along the Matanuska, July,
I sit in midnight dusk
Amidst low flight of eagles, gulls
On sand bars weaved into the cold
River's braid, grey with the
Silt of many cliff bank rains
& think of her in snow white
Gown marrying today, far away,
Who once lived with me. Will
It last? What do I know—my
Heart's serene isolation complete,
This sun above that will not set—
Let it on waters go pink sky.
All love's desire here inside.

Palmer, Alaska
22 July 1995

SUSITNA RIVER MEDITATION

Drunken forests disappear in high fog.
Fields of cottongrass in lowlands dance.

Loon stands on head again & again.
Moose coat darkens wet spruce brown.

Bear wander the old blueberry trails.
Caribou routes pass beyond to the north.

Terns & eagles hunt Crooked Creek.
Monks-hood & willow for miles & miles.

A million rainbow come & go.
Only silence never dies.

Alaska Range
26-28 July 1995

HOPE POINT

No switchbacks to Hope Point.
Meadows rise almost vertical.
Red & white baneberry, alder & fir.
Screeching merlin, cranberry brush.
Yellow paintbrush, yellow ferns.
Heather fresh as earth's first winter snow.
Raven wings in tattered black.
Purple harebell, midnight sun.
White fog sleeps on knife edge rock.
Hoarse waves sob for wind-blown grass.

1 August 1995

SACRED CLOWN

for Lawrence Giles

He walks up tragic 4th Street—brooding, withdrawn,
Pondering the ponderosities of his ponderings
'Neath black stringy hair hanging down, head lowered,
To study ants on sidewalk, downtown Anchorage,

Where now Russians in traditional orthodox spooky Muscovite garb
Tout suitcases of beer & tourists mill sadly through Woolworth's
Cinnamon bears & french fries & keychains & bleak vinyl shower curtains,
Corner of F, past winos face-down on grass-roofed cabin & cops
Pointing to a blind couple tapping their earnest canes in front of dreary
Federal Building guard with blue shirted sunlit face—

& him filing mute past the sagging benches of obese despair,
Past the drunk Inuit woman, cigarette in her outstretched hand shouting,
"Why me, why me Lord, why me, why why why me,"
Through thick snowmobile-bride wedding cake tears,

Past the tall man with plastered smile
Bent over a baby sparrow lost maybe like the bird who danced so high
He became the North Star above these solemn & obscure
& unruly distant peaks & glaciers—

Above him angels that remember when the yellow poppies fell
From the Big Dipper & took over making dreams instead of music
Or the brown pulleys of saltwater lifting soft rivers of fog—
All the while thru chintzy eyeglasses, the left frame without any lens,
Drifting effortlessly within his solitary & immeasurable heart.

3 August 1995

GREEN RIVER AT DINOSAUR

Great grandmother moon stands barefoot.
Clouds look like an elk's spine, broke.
Slowly I walk into the fast current.
Cottonwoods line the opposite shore.
No one can see me in the darkness.
Naked I stand in the dark blue river.
I wade into the velvety never ending universe
  of dying things.
What exists that makes this noise?

9 August 1995

INTERPRETING THE PETROGLYPHS AT DELUGE SHELTER

for Chris Ballerano

This is the bridge the people crossed
When they left the animals & their language
& their devotion to the Four Directions
Of the Sacred Earth.

There is the Elder holding the hand of
The children of the people above the crack
In the rock wall, Long Ears the Elder,
Bending his long ears toward the animals—

& the Antler'd One, the Many Antler'd Elder,
Turning his rack toward Elder Long Ears,
All the children of the animals below the crack
In the rock wall & visible to whomever passes.

Jones Hole Creek
10 August 1995

ELY CREEK

Bighorn sheep bed down at dusk.
Buddha sits in high red sandstone cave.
Three magpies land in moon-white grass.
From above, a cougar watches me.

How many fires have bared this ground?
Juniper & Old Sage calm the heart.
Sudden waterfalls appear in rain.
Deer stand motionless & then move on.

11 August 1995

ARAPAHO PASS, MID-AUGUST

The rocks want to be grass
    & the grass wants to be stone.
Falcon sweeps from behind a ridge.
    Campfires lie beneath summer hail.
Bees dream of roses.
    Bluebells of storms.
Soon, I'll be like the man
    Who never walked the earth.

19 August 1995

SOMETHING SUMMER SAID

who stole my life?
where did it go?
into the tiny
books of milkweed?
a beehive of fog?
it's supposed to snow.
your smile makes me cry.
i watch you follow
the sunflowers home.

September 1995

Wild Basin

NEW YEAR'S SERMON

In his youth, the rabbi had conducted
memorable new year services. He retold &
reinterpreted the old story of Abraham &
Isaac in light of the Arabs, the Blacks,
Israel, the Republican Party, Hitler & the
Exodus. The cantors came & went, the
shofar blew. Lands were traded. Hostages
taken. The years passed like rocks & bullets
& the blossoming olives & poppies across
the desert hills. The story of the father's
near-killing of his son only brought painful
memories—my poor mad father pulling his
knife on me as a boy—sacrificed to his own
mad god. So frail now, the rabbi'd become,
barely able to lift the scrolls over his head,
losing his place, the sermon incoherent,
the congregants talking, pointing at him.

25 September 1995

UNDIVIDED ATTENTION

when you spoke to me
i did not revere the bones of your
unbearable clowns,
        their myriad futures
                    crumbling in blue jails
like a rusted saxophone
of gods with gold teeth.

                    whoever you are
you have my attention,
take it all in.
tell me again about
untrue eyes & prostitute balls.
tell me of demons,
        i'll say that they're flowers
                    in the purple moonlight
of claustrophobic heartache
where notorious masked welders
torch our dreams
in enormous & bleak & auctorial
chopshops of the soul's dark face,
        its chases & wrecks
                & corpse-posed shadows.

                        whoever you are
skeleton born of skeletal cloth
where the eyeliner
of abandoned skulls
washes you away like
a hurricane made of glass—
        don't let me interrupt
                    your fatal immense costume.
unpersuadable, relentless,
i'll say that sorrow
is not rooted
anywhere.

                                29 October 1995

A CONVERSATION WITH MY HEART AFTER THE ASSASSINATION OF YITZHAK RABIN

My heart, my faceless heart,
You are the desert clouds that bury
Their mother in the stones.
I am a child who cannot see wonder.
I am a child, lost on the street.
You are the green olive tree cut down.
You are all that is vulnerable.
The future coughing up yellow blood.
Snow that gives itself to Hate.
You climb up the steep marrow of never.
Nothing goes unfinished eternal.
Only this body in which you took refuge
Falls, chained to the purple air.

13 November 1995

ON THE DAY MY BASIC SKILLS ENGLISH CLASS FINISHED READING *TO KILL A MOCKINGBIRD*

Maria had another one of those dreams about
The 30-year-old man who raped her last year.
Constance writes a letter to Boo Radley
Asking him if the blue dusk is God's T-shirt.
Venezuela opens up about his mother's coke habit.
Shantrelle thinks that 20 years from now
She'll still remember who Tom Robinson is.
Hezikiah & his cousins pile into the old Ford wagon
To see his father before they pull the plug.
Fantasia designs the poster for the United Colors
Party on Saturday night in memory of Dawn—
The girl killed in last weekend's head-on wreck.
Bobby gets an escort in cuffs from the school.
Cube sees anyone who's poor as a mockingbird.

14 November 1995

CAN DRIVE

When Lauren's here, we listen to Jane Siberry.
She says she's not afraid of the bliss love brings.

At night, I pass the highschool boys with their
Recipes for pipebombs, the girls with ideograms
On their necks & labias pierced with rubies.

Holly's far off in a crimelab trying to solve
The case of an unidentifiable drifter wearing
Either a nightshirt or a morning gown
Killed by a broken rainbow.

I learn who you are & watch you learn to see
Between memory & hatred & forgiveness & nothing.

The naked world burns $100 bills in the darkness.
Anonymous, I'm like a can drive at Thanksgiving.

I do not lick the ground looking for dead bodies.

Why is it that when I want you there is no one?

20 November 1995

TO KNOW YOU AS YOU KNOW YOURSELF

for Mark Rennick

As you know yourself I know you.
As your angels know you.
The way they speak to you.

As waves crash you are waves
& I am waves breaking on the shore.
The way each wave is smote down.

As you will never be the same again.
The way each wave rises on high.
So I am never the same again.

As you are fear's perfect freedom
& none taunt you from yourself
So I am untaunted from myself.

Salmon Creek
25 December 1995

WOOD

Everything enters this change with you.
A white ray falling from the darkened sky.
Hours full of silver & sunshine near rivers.
The tenderness of Bodies aching for love.

The inner connects to the outer tree.
You align yourself to the wood to come.
Weak & strong enter this change with you.
Those crazy with the loneliness of the land.

Who gaze at axe handles till they rot.
Those from whom you wish never to part.
All the caresses deep mountains cannot hide.
Those left behind like fallen trees.

6 January 1996

THE NEXT DAY

We speak in kisses—
  the white stairway of kisses.

Our kisses speak like peach trees
  through corridors of secret birds

                that dwell near the purple river
        where seasons crumble
        like a child falling
off the moon.

For a thousand miles our kisses speak,
  making pathless ways for what arrives.

All the next day your breath on mine.
  On the empty streets of kisses.

1 February 1996

LUKASA

The only thing I can remember is the beautiful—
Looking for water from a deeper well.
The cottonwoods with songs that travel over prairie
& the many ghosts that live in old fences.

All I remember is the beautiful—
Green sunflowers worn thin by the moon.
The young man who dresses himself like a bride.

Hands with seventeen fingers.
The spines of roses & wolves at Yellowstone.
Only the beautiful I remember—

The black sounds of roots definitive as childbirth.
The certainty of love & being understood.
That which breaks open the clouds.

One returns to the self as if to the beautiful.

22 February 1996

AFTER MY CAR IS TOTALED IN A ROCKSLIDE

My throat sleeps like an avalanche
With modems & social workers
Vaccinating the homeless in tunnels
Filled with drums & fire escapes.

In my knees mechanics inspect flowers &
Gas tanks on lifts made of violins.
Behind the lacquered red toolboxes of my legs
An unshaven astronomer chases one-eyed pigeons
Through alleys of glamorous & sullen tires.

Windshields shatter in my gloves.
My ankles are manuscripts made of radiators
& the casings of split-open transmissions
Bent like half-folded wheelchairs creaking
With all the demons of my wrongdoings
Rising through the floorboards.

My teeth are tiles from the roofs of
Suicide bombers exploding straight up
& the rocks that fall upon the highway
Crush the cellular telephones of my wrists.

Vail Pass
11 March 1996

SHEKHINA

Only for a while do we warm ourselves
With flowers & bluebirds & grieving.

Shekhina, you are the midwife of illness
& weddings & all that is sparks & pregnant
& all that is elbows & kisses & semen.

You accompany exile's wretched longing
To consummate the soul's deep-plum sunken glee.

You are all that is lightheadedness & insomnia
& that which is missing & that which reveals
Wherever we were, whatever planet.

Your voice is that of a sick person,
A dried-up sea, the dark furniture of sighs,
The melancholy elegance of rusted piers
& light which is always changing, always fleeting,

The sun that rakes the sidewalk in geometries
Of impossibly thin shadows
That glide into the orange dusk,

Into the inner chambers & inner sanctums
Winged & nude & beyond the remoteness of
The iron shouting of the world.

In the vagina of centuries,
Your body is an alphabet of blood
& quarantines & testicles & pent-up sobs,
Candles & thick milk, the bread of thighs,

The alabaster smell of humility, ribs,
Black lightning, the hooves of silence concealed
Within the concealed of the concealed within.

It is you who carry us to the sapphire mountains,
You whose feet go down to death.

Nowhere on earth is void of your gown of erections.
You are the hours & weeks yoked to honey & bandages,
The elegance of hovels, the mansions of poverty.
When cities tremble with rain, it is you speaking—

Filling that impossible distance between solitude's
Round flaming window of amorous throbbing,

Its ladders & palaces that float by & arms of pain
& realms of repentance & realms of copulation.

Abrupt, you lean against the roots of air
As we choose something personal,
Something mutual, something indescribable,

& opening to every crevice, every uncharted beloved
That falls through the skin
Of the violet tides of our frenzied nothingness.

In the wet green rhythm at the heart of absence,
It is you who knows the violence that comes
To each life, who touches us
When we wished to die, when we wanted to live.

As we remember the face of weeping
You are here like a synagogue made from a dress,

Like a mother waking up in the middle of the night
To bake a dark creamy-brown chocolate cake.

When we lie down in dust,
You are the dust of premonitions
From where begins our love over again.

18 February-
18 March 1996

REINCARNATION

Mudra upon mudra. A voice more gentle than thought. Like tolerance but more generous than farm villages of the prehistoric Near East. More definitive Sumerians with their sun-dried cuneiforms & horizontal lines. Hieroglyphics' mature Egyptian be-bob 3050 BC. The entire Library of Congress on a disk the size of a penny. Bardo Libraries. Library implants. All the velocity & misfortune of grapes, shattered oceans & Semitic pianos in the Greek vowels of night with their secret zambooky arteries behind the ear that do not tremble until the hour of death. Like Hoboken in 1983, without knowing what happened to one another, we meet in a forest looking for the path out of the woods. I cannot tell you the way, but I can point out the ways that lead further into the thicket.

30 April 1996

DREAM OF MY FATHER IN UNIFORM

In a dream my father came to me after 35 years.
He wanted to explain why he'd been discharged by the
Army dishonorably. "Yeah, I started fights," he said,
"disobeyed orders my superiors gave. I was a misfit,
renegade bad-ass Jew sick of living in *Olam ha-Tohu*,
the World of Confusion. It was tough enough being
German, that betrayal broke me young. It followed me
down the streets & in the schools & moviehouses &
parks along the lake. Into the stores, wherever I
worked it followed me. The holocaust never happened.
The yids were the true aggressors. It was the Zionists
that sold out their own people to leverage Palestine.
The rabbi turned down two million dollars from the
Gestapo in exchange for the liberation of the camps.
Always envy, jealousy & envy & talk about money—
I've heard it my whole life. In times of trouble you'll
hear it too. They own Hollywood, the media, the
newspapers. Their usury is like cancer eating away
at governments & militaries & the teachings in the
universities & the laws of the courts." Then, descending
through the floorboards, he said, "Though I have
avoided you these many years, thinking we would never
see each other again, overpowered by the fears I've
hid, I have been given this opportunity."

19 May 1996

MEDITATION AT A STOPLIGHT IN THE RAIN

Empty streets after midnight—
Like the dark blue wings of the bank swallow
Drowned in crimson
& I'm walking slowly nowhere—scornful, laughing
At sleepless cars with tiny breadcrumb mirrors
& Amusement Park shoes scattered like depression
Through the sage gloved Moonlight parade.

Everything is timeless—
Stars flowing within endless rivers of Protests &
Weeping & houses filled with the poor.
The rain—a scorched blue ferris wheel
Typing out carnivals with her fingers
Like red glass clocks with four hands & the alarm
In ourselves passing out of eternity.

As the rain is to sleep,
So the rain agrees to live in the wet-sock silence
Of intersections, halting the endless steps
Of those who already know so much of everything
That approaches with the disordered fury
To live again—
Like a brown spaceship landing in your soul.

The rain will be a lost face in the mist of an hour
As it hovers overhead,
Chanting like an insect in a greenhouse.
Why do I remain
When all I see is the grey October eyes of those
Whom made me feel I was loved,
But then I awaken & there's no one here.

1 October 1997

Oh-Be-Joyful

THE HUMMINGBIRDS

There were hummingbirds & young children
And then Donna appeared, without her husband
From behind the door that tears had shut.
It was Sunday. There was a treehouse &
A bedroll in the hayloft above the stables.
After so many years, so many hours watching
The mind, its tricks & magic, I yearned
Simply for the vertical rivers of timelessness
That come like death to the heart, release it
& throw us off the cliffs of emotion that we
May fall upwards through each specific change.
I understood ascension that day, seeing her
Transformed by the 3006 feelings of movement.
Gone, hidden, she was in the blue iris.
She was in the blue that climbs into the sky.
All so we could meet in that moment—our
Ghosts that wept ghostly in their peace & we
Who remain beneath hummingbird wings.

Geneseo, New York
2 June 1996

ON A BUS STALLED IN TRAFFIC NEAR THE GOLDEN GATE BRIDGE

Fast clouds. All the mystery of the sea & her lover so restless &
sweeping & bleak & inside the same head. Strange wild lightning
beyond the glow-in-the-dark necklaces of sleeping children &
boys with cherry lollipops, silver-capped teeth & legs spread
out casual gazing at the Alcatraz lighthouse with the sudden
goneness of little lavender men's prayers in the sugarbowl of
loneliness. The grey donut baker. Air conditioning repairman.
Bouncer at a topless bar. Lucy, who saw snow in Reno for the
first time. A sad rucksack tucked behind seat patched & patched
again & repatched like all the sighs in the world. A single
mother who makes recordings telling what time movies begin.
The painter who used to paint flowers & now in corner of a
cemetery paints a rooster calling for his friends to wake. Then
there is the renowned archer who has never, not even in bril-
liant daylight, hit the target & he is kneeling silently in the dirt
swarmed by yellow butterflies blown in from the bay.

24 June 1996

WITNESS NO. 87

One 15-year-old, Witness No. 87,
Was taken prisoner in July 1992
& raped by four men.

Over the following two weeks
She was gang raped every evening.
She endured rapes for eight months.

She & other women kept house
For soldiers in the day
& were raped at night.

On Feb. 25, 1993, Radomir Kovac
Sold her for 500 German marks to
Two soldiers from Montenegro.

28 June 1996

PRAJNA OF THE DARK AGE

after Jack Kerouac

In the prajna of the Dark Age
I remember your hands,
Your lips like marijuana
& hair like feedback.

Less you forget what your eyes saw
Everything appears
Amid invasions & maternity
& the swift destruction of gangs
Their handsigns & colors
Clothed in flesh,

In a singular love & understanding
That ascends from the earth
As the sun rolls on
Through the Dark Age.

You journey to me & where do I journey?
I journey & journey continually,
Like a ghost leaving his cigarette
Burning in the torchlight of prajna.

1 July 1996

THE BRIDE'S MAID & THE BRIDE

The women gather around the bride
As is the custom before a wedding,

Except in this coming together, there is
No singing or dancing in her honor,

Only the sadness of the bride
& her tear-stained dress.

Her maid struck dead by lightning
Next to her on backcountry trail—
I've no right to be happy let alone alive.

It's all they can do to keep her nails
From rending the lace

& in the final moments before she weds,
To hide her tears with veils.

14 July 1996

OH-BE-JOYFUL

After wading cold Slate Creek
Up the valley I begin with its waterfalls
& trees torn out by the roots & talking leaves.
There's room for every bluebell, every bend
In the pounding of white water over stones.
A traveler on the ancient route, I wanted
To be real, but I don't know if I was.
In my heart there were asters,
Cities of butterflies & yellow hummingbirds,
Even Purple Peak after the lightning
Begins its search, its lonesome search
Across mountains in its walking bones,
Clattering up & down Oh-Be-Joyful Pass.

17 July 1996

PROMISED LAND

Promised Land hitches Highway 64 everyday
between Farmington & Shiprock. Just out of his
prison shoes after his fourth DWI, some nights
he sleeps at Bob's Car Wash in one of the stalls
where it's almost a room with a swamp cooler.
The other weavers, that's what he calls drunks,
steal the groceries that he's taking home for
his daughter. The weavers steal his carton of
eggs & bread & cheese. He sees his ex from time
to time selling herself for a can of hairspray
& a bottle—she's never seen their daughter
since day one. His mother's a drunken whore.
His father, a drunk, got run over in Teec Nos
Pos when he was sixteen. Promised Land knows
what it comes down to. The dreams not finished.
That's his place back there with the pink trailers,
rabbits, upside-down piano, City Market &
Little Caesars—just beyond the bridge over the
San Juan River, the muddy San Juan. Promised
Land'll tell you all about that rusty silver bridge.
How he dropped from the girders onto trucks
Rolling by. How he leapt into the river those
Long summers past.

Shiprock, Navajoland,
20 July 1996

BETATAKIN MEDITATION

A 13th century Pueblo farmer cut these
Handholds in stone, these ladders of fir.
His corn is stored on high Betatakin cliff.
This ground he turns with a sturdy hoe.
Water's drawn from a clear cold stream.
The wind hurries him on & will not wait.
How would he feel to see the world in ruins
Wrecked & broken beyond belief?
Though a thousand clues he leaves behind
Morning after morning flowers bloom & fade.

21 July 1996

RUINS

What ruins lie within you—
Which are war ruins, which the ruins of love without end.
A fragrant sage-cracked & peeling riverbottom.

The ruin of language, the ruin of silence.
The childhood handed down through the ruins of hours.
Yourself & myself, the ruin of desire.

All that's beyond ruin—making up for affection lost.
In ruins, who you were not.
Who you clung to thought after thought.

The mute smile rising from the ruins you were.
Beings once clad in garments so bright.
The ruins of hair & headdresses & looms.

Agony's ruins, from ruins' ruin unbound.
The silence of granaries & potteries & yellow towers in the sun.
Skeleton Mesa falling down canyons of blood.

A million ruins in the high cliffs of each heart.
The ruin of handprints chipping off the dark.
Ruins that bring forth the good future you start.

28 July 1996

DOMESTIC TERROR COUPLETS

How much can a generation suffer?
Crown glories in tourniquet shadows.

Stories expressed but never told
As we rushed from nowhere to nowhere

Like Sisyphus carrying a huge vanity radio
Uphill in search of love.

Am I supposed to write songs to praise
The end of Civil Rights—

Encourage people to burn churches
& make instant craters in our streets?

Travel across this land calling
Women & men to join

This movement of domestic terror—
Its pipedreams & pipebombs.

Its headless dolls, twisted metals
& bodies shattered like downtown lights.

1 August 1996

MINE IS THE ROLLING ON THAT LIES BENEATH WHAT YOU HEARD

Follow the desert poppies & prairie grass.
Pass the corn so high in August lowlands.
The sunflower fields of Nebraska
Mingle with the cool of the evening dew.
Who sets this table before me
In the presence of my energies?
Mine is the rolling on that lies
Beneath what you heard.
& if you never desire my heart's communion
Then my universe shall exist alongside
Your universe.
My time with beauty, the smell of a rose,
Alongside your own Beauty meditation.
My doubt alongside yours.
The joy rooted in a raindrop, a single raindrop,
Splashing down upon your tender belly,
Sliding down low alongside my joy.

North Platte
to Mississippi River
3-4 August 1996

THE FIREFLIES OF CLEVELAND

The man & woman
return to the old
elm tree where

they met years ago.

The lake is covered
with a layer of algae

thin as the sundress
she wore that afternoon.

The last colors
of the day
are the blues

on the wings
of a pair of heron
flying together
into the reeds.

Trembling
in the understory,
they kiss,

surrounded
by the light
of many fireflies.

5 August 1996

IN MEMORY OF ROBERT DUNCAN

for Morgan Jarema

After knowledge, the next important thing is Robert Duncan's "What Do I Know Of The Old Lore?" Then, fudgicles, stately Wayne Manor, a box full of retinas, the last issue of *Planet Detroit*. After that, gold painted macaroni jewelry, Apollinaire urinating at the end of "Zone," Monet's garden, the making of gardens as a way to prepare one's death, the weight of mountains, cosmic intoxication, a giant with a bag of stones. Next is a prince rowing in a sewer, an actress running thru the flooded streets with a victrola in flames, the great vowels & narrow chasm of sentences from which fallen celestials ascend, *Mystery Science Theater 3000*, children asleep in the newspaper light of dawn—their thin exquisite feet sticking out from blankets where they dream of diamond grasshoppers hiding in chandeliers & fishtanks & sparrows in birdbaths & tigers in the kingdom of a sailor moon. Then comes "Our nada who art in nada...," a circus in a flood, a transvestite palm reader predicting the day Herbert Huncke died in New York, Italian ice at Asbury Park, the Fillmore West, soldiers home from the war listening to friends shout, "Don't go, man. Don't go back there!" After that, polar bears in New Orleans, robotic arm wrestling, a winter heat wave, Robbie Robertson's "American Roulette," the Santa Claus of Greco-erotica, a Dead Sea Scrolls ashtray, accordion orchestras, burials where nobody comes, flowers for a girl who last night had a vision of the sea & in the morning her boyfriend borrowed a car & without a word, chauffeured her blindfolded to the Rockaways.

Grand Rapids
10 August 1996

NISHNABOTRA RIVER

Rolling hills, dark folds of land.
Not even the golden light of August makes him stay.
The corn never stays no matter which dress
    you wear Nishnabotra.
No matter how good your hair smells Nishnabotra,
    the sweet yellow corn never stays too long.
Every year it happens like this.
Every year it happens like this.
        He returns to the night sky
            filling the sky with stars.

                    Council Bluffs
                    11 August 1996

EXCARNATE

after Basho

It is a strange kind of possession—
Being seen thru.

As snowflakes frozen into the lake
Are seen thru ice
& the necks of geese
above the marshgrass.

How the inside of a juniper
Twists itself to the outside.
The quiet way trees do not laugh in winter.
Their skin trembling with vowels of stone.

Ask me anything you want.
The bears are green, the apples black.
You smell like icicles
On ancient dwarf pine.

The bindings shall not really bind.

Deep as the snow is
Let me go as far as I can.

Nelson, British Columbia
16 November 1996

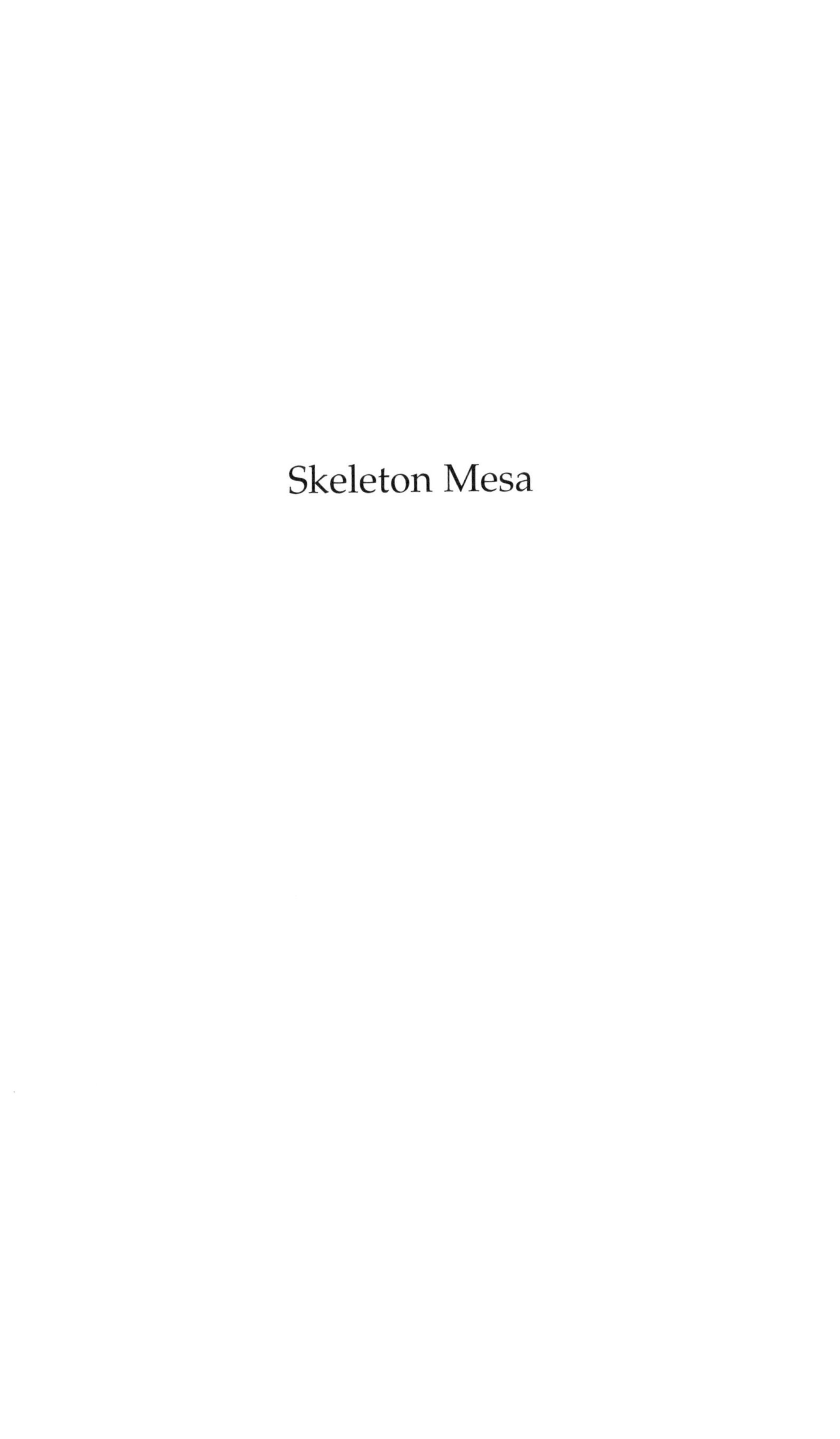

Skeleton Mesa

ODE TO IMPERMANENCE

for Suzanne Down

Impermanence, getting out of her Jaguar at midnight. The lovers walking away even before they know they're leaving. Sam Shepard in *Voyager*.

Is it all we have—to press the words against the higher ground of autumn leaves & GulfLINK news from Kamisiyah, the milkweed like Ed Wood flying saucers caught in trees, the light on the Third Flatiron at dusk, Frank Sinatra turning off the windshield wipers in *Young At Heart?*

The fall of the Arapaho. The fall of the Kiowa. The wisdom of barn swallows in a quilted maple sky. Thoreau starring in many French movies, starting the revolution in Czechoslovakia, drinking with the plumbers in the library at Alexandria. Brigitte Bardot in *Viva Maria!*

Then everything is still & finally, the path takes on the undisturbed sheen of Orion's sword.

21 November 1996

O HOMELESS VETERANS OF WARS AROUND THE PLANET

after Sam Abrams

Ye trained killers, homeless vets, come home like a hat after a stampede
To graffitied dumpsters & graffitied alleys mumbling encyclopedias of
Winter coats, quarters, stale bread & orchestras at funerals—

I chain my meat wheel body to your epithalium of rats & shadows,
Automobile grime of buses & stretch limos & taxis & the cars of the rich
& the cars of the poor that darken the One Way sign.

When others can use long distance like therapy,
You carry a word around for months like *legerdemain,* the light of hands,
& lyrics, like Phil Och's "Crucifixion"
& the Banner Spangled Star which you say to yourself
For all the dead men floating down rivers.

27 November 1996

LIKE BUDDHA WALKING HOME
FROM THE CARNIVAL

is the low flight of a marsh hawk
over the hands of three laughing women
            till a man with thin black gloves
     passes by.

slowly arcing over the white horse
curled alongside
       prairie dog hole
          cockleburs in its mane.

the purple grass, limestone cliffs.
over the deer who waded to island grass.
          miniature nests of snow
    in a crook of twigs.

the long shadows of blue geese.
skeleton of butterflies in a ditch.
       the painter at his easel mixing colors
  all day.

          over the bees & thistle
      the creekside milkweed
like a hysterectomy,
  an empty doll house.

over two old brothers
 in a beat up truck.
   the fenceposts like statues
         that do not know me.

over tiny stones
frozen to the surface
at the edge of
the pond.

28 November 1996

RUBRIC

These are the standards for tomorrow's lessons—
The student will spark, blaze, create a wall of flame.

The student will genesis life on foreign planets
Immediately & immediately & so immediately
     like Epimethius.

Like a Turkish international freeze deterrent
& the sudden appearance of Noh players
     with Johnny Cash in the scarlet analogue
          balcony tanager Yangtse Three Gorge choir.

The student will count the stars, count the plagues,
Count the wars, count the sorrows, count the bones.

The student will articulate with cyborg depression
Like Nebraska to Michigan & angels with sponge implants—
     Spanish botany memories iconic he
          & unverifiable Margery on sax
       while sentences of green trumpets burst
       upon the orioles of love.

The student will be very sad, like a catalog store.
Like donations elaborated upon emeralds & pianos
       dying of cancer in your purple envelope.

5 December 1996

TEN MENORAHS

On the third night of Hanukkah, he lights the ten
menorahs in his room & prays for the suicidal & impoverished
& those who butcher neighbors & those left for dead under
piles of rotting corpses, for the people of China & India &
Pakistan, Rwanda & Tibet, for the peoples of Hebron & Belgrade,
for those who steal elections, for those owned by central
intelligence, for those alone in marriage, those addicted to
power, those who walk barefoot over mountains, those beaten
by police, cheated from justice, without jobs, money, hope, forgot,
shamed by today's global war, those living without vision, never
present in the moment, those with chemical therapies in their
bodies, those with a very old woman inside a cave within their
bodies welcoming foreign chemicals to do battle with disease,
those who weep like candles burning down, those who await
you, poet of the future, who sit in jails & courts & schools &
jobs & space station corners where the check is never enough,
where the presents never get bought, where only the fleet of
stoned dope rockets go, where only the dictator's voice is
heard.

8 December 1996

DECEMBER SPEEDS BY

December speeds by like teenage self-abuse & parents with no
Money for doctors & Canada with its thousand feet of snow &
Impossible lessons of refugees pleading like Woody Guthrie

After his sister lit her dress on fire & Elvis praying to his twin
brother for guidance & teachers with wings like plutonium
weeping for the sadness in their students' eyes.

December, like an incessant bell at dusk & a stone by the door
& bales of alfalfa wrapped with red ribbon by Uruguay girls
Surrounded by police & knowing there is no misery in life.

                                        12 December 1996

DEDICATED TO THE QUALITY OF PATIENCE

Dedicated to the quality of patience,
I had a dream of a sex palace. You weren't
Wearing too much, just your green hair & rings.
Yellow lariats hooped over a bed under a waterfall
Near where you fell through the crust waist deep.
Nine crimson suitcases were packed with explosives.
The pink suitcase with crisp hundred dollar bills.
You were walking thru deep snow
When an Australian woman found you
Fixing your hair in a bun with an icicle.
Thru the satin-dressed marionette trees
The dried flowers of the apples
Press against the journals
Of our winter morning thoughts.
Your legs were wet, your torn jeans soaked through
From walking long & hard.

16 December 1996

THE HALF-LIFE OF SURRENDER

> Engaged at a
> dance after driving up from a reading in Manhattan.
A cake made of thalidomide on the front seat
Of a pink-finned '58 Cadillac spewing black
Leukemiac promises as if they were black carnations
& cliffs of myself remembering there was an inside
She loved in silence.
> That desired life endured even though only as
Repetition & the not repeat of the errors of family & the errors
In letting it in until the theater manager turned on the house
Lights before the credits were over or the walls of cassettes of
High school basketball games that nothing was stronger than
Lost strength without ever really.
> In the chronic inflammatory solitude of
Bingo hall luncheonettes, only serenity was real, serenity &
Going over Niagara Falls in a skull overflowing with the halflife
Of surrender—its robins & magpies in the gloves of shadows on
Concrete medians of starlit highways twisting around the
Orangeade mountains of astro quadroonery.
> There were the white boxcars
& the emerald switchblade headaches of a virgin with overcoat
Eyes. And when you wrote me of your rage & your pile of *MS.*
Magazines soaked in lighter fluid, it set off a series of electric
Chairs in the dumpsters near where the addict was drinking
From a toilet bowl on Christmas Eve.

25 December 1996

HAVE TO CUT OUR VISIT SHORT

The Visit approached like an airplane with the skin of
a beaver landing in a field where horses graze, their
steamy breath rising to heaven in corrals rung by bees
& sleeping lilacs & willows with their buds like icing on
sweet rolls. The Visit descended upon them the way
rivers wed ice in the crystalline structure of each
moment's glass slipper, by its weight sinking beneath
the surface of rivers & the splitting of cottonwoods &
their inevitable falling & the immeasurable narrowing
of ponds when covered with ice. It loomed like a child's
shallow kisses with magpies circling. Like a wife who
had lost her way in the winter of marriage. The Visit
was a door in the bend of a river slamming open &
shut & then ripped off its hinges of thistle & mint.
The Visit was an empty swirl of sad useless grass
clocks ticking out the hours of deer along cliffs in a
secret language conceived like Nuremberg & Ouray
& Kansas City where the other meaning of The Gate
is unlocked by the Master of Hearts flying from the
starship of bones & pelts & masks in the tangerine
searchlight of a pure individual freedom where it is
clear that grace & lucidity would not fail the cosmos.

17 January 1997

DANCING LAST NIGHT

All this talk of Zajedno (Unity)—
Still, my life is like Robert De Niro's in *The Fan*.

The low waving grass in the wind is my only happiness.
Some days I remember my wife & wish I were dead.
Cactus flattened by snow, that's my spirit tonight.

Sparrow cleans beak on forsythia twig.
Crows on traffic signals are like big black staplers.

You dance so close yet I am nothing to you.
The room is crowded but I dance alone.

1 February 1997

CAN'T DOWNSIZE THE VOID

Can't downsize the void.
No cost-of-living rises in benefits to cut there.
Can't cremate it like Gandhi's bones.
No ashes to forget 10,000,000 years.

Can't fight proxy wars in the void.
Can't topple kings, explicate political mayhem.
No public letters, no number 2 official.
No families reunited in the void.

No workers sent to pulse limbo.
Can't compromise over World Trade.
Revisit old dingy punishment cell.
Can't hear the Pope's mass from the void.

No marijuana studies. No 'Thin' drugs.
No Lady of the Broom sweeping up broken glass.
No serial bombers, No Carnival Air.
Can't rush paperbacks into print in the void.

Can't admit failure to improve computers.
No help for Inner-City residents planned.
Can't ask to review blood evidence.
No crime labs to fault in the void.

Demonstrators march thousands of millennia unseen.
Billions upon billions in charity never bring aid.
No role for Evil. No factory doors closed.
Can't legislate anonymity & selflessness in the void.

2 February 1997

"SHOULDN'T HAVE TO DO THIS"

     "I shouldn't have to do this," says the rabbi
at the graveside, bending down to kiss the casket
in his red skullcap. "Even though he was old &
sick, even though it was his time to go and I have
conducted funeral after funeral, even though I have
led the mourner's prayer for his wife, for my own—
this is no small task . . . so very few of us remain &
I'd always assumed it would be him where now I
stand, saying these words over me . . . But now
you're dead, my oldest friend & with you the world I
know lies now beneath these feet . . .

                          24 February 1997

I TOOK A DUMP IN THE BATHROOM OF PAIN

The whole earth is balanced upon
Animals teaching themselves joy.
Yahna stopped by with her fingers like violets.
Who'd slash the wrists of your self-esteem?

The merest aspects of being human
Elevate us to the beautiful whole that is.
How simply you return to yourself—
Like the white leaves of the brittlebrush.

Who is it that again must begin this new life?
John Lee Hooker at a shaded tinaja.
Buffalo Springfield at Monterey.
We love & we lose but only among the living.

1 March 1997

The Author

Jim Cohn attended the legendary Jack Kerouac School of Disembodied Poetics. After years of investigation into the signing space of Deaf ASL iconography and skillful means practice in the realm of visible & invisible body-linked discourse, he worked towards the establishment of a Disability Literature Canon based upon the heritage of ongoing individual liminal composition. The editor and publisher of *Napalm Health Spa*, as well as a recording artist who fused bardic spoken word and roots music traditions learned from collaboration with Allen Ginsberg, he founded the Museum of American Poetics in 1997 as a living memorial to the candor & spirit of experimentation, healing, perseverance, openness and compassion transmitted by the masters of the Beat Generation. *The Dance Of Yellow Lightning Over The Ridge* is his third collection of poetry, along with *Green Sky, Prairie Falcon* and *Grasslands,* in a longer work-in-progress entitled *The One Great Poem,*